ROBERT BROWNING

on

Love

ROBERT BROWNING

on

Love

EDITED BY

Stephen Brennan

Skyhorse Publishing

Copyright © 2016 by Stephen Brennan

Art credits:
Shutterstock/tukkki, page viii
Shutterstock/Olga Korneeva, page 16
Shutterstock/Ajuga, page 40
Shutterstock/DeMih, page 62
Shutterstock/Labetskiy Alexandr, page 96
Shutterstock/Nataliia Litovchenko, page 114
Shutterstock/mamita, page 136
Shutterstock/Baleika Tamara, page 156

Skyhorse Publishing books may be purchased in bulk at special discounts for sales promotion, corporate gifts, fund-raising, or educational purposes. Special editions can also be created to specifications. For details, contact the Special Sales Department, Skyhorse Publishing, 307 West 36th Street, 11th Floor, New York, NY 10018 or info@skyhorsepublishing.com.

Skyhorse® and Skyhorse Publishing® are registered trademarks of Skyhorse Publishing, Inc.®, a Delaware corporation.

Visit our website at www.skyhorsepublishing.com.

10 9 8 7 6 5 4 3 2 1

Library of Congress Cataloging-in-Publication Data is available on file.

Cover design by Jane Sheppard
Cover photo by Shutterstock

Print ISBN: 978-1-63450-239-9
Ebook ISBN: 978-1-63450-886-5

Printed in the United States of America

Contents

You will only expect a few words, what will those be?

When the heart is full it may run over, but the real
fullness stays within.

Words can never tell you, however, form them,
transform them anyway, how perfectly dear you are to
me, perfectly dear to my heart and soul.

I look back, and in every one point, every word and
gesture, every letter, every silence, you have been
entirely perfect to me, I would not change
one word, one look.

My hope and aim are to preserve this love, not to fall
from it, for which I trust to God who procured it for
me, and doubtless can preserve it.

You have given me the highest, completest proof of
love that ever one human being gave another.

I am all gratitude, and all pride (under the proper
feeling which ascribes pride to the right source) all
pride that my life has been so crowned by you.

—Letter to Elizabeth Barrett Browning
on the occasion of their marriage

Love's
Desire

That fawn-skin-dappled hair of hers,
And the blue eye
Dear and dewy,
And that infantine fresh air of hers!

—*A Pretty Woman*

***

She would succeed in her absurd attempt,
And fascinate by sinning, show herself

—*Pippa Passes*

***

"At last thou art come! Ere I tell, ere thou speak,
Kiss my cheek, wish me well!" Then I wished it, and
did kiss his cheek.

—*Saul*

She should never have looked at me
If she meant I should not love her!

—*Cristina*

A soft and easy life these ladies lead:
Whiteness in us were wonderful indeed.
Oh, save that brow its virgin dimness,
Keep that foot its lady primness,
Let those ankles never swerve
From their exquisite reserve,
Yet have to trip along the streets like me,
All but naked to the knee!

—*In Three Days*

Give her but a least excuse to love me!

—*Pippa Passes*

Love's Desire

Each enjoys
Its night so well, you cannot break
The sport up, so, indeed must make
More stay with me, for others' sake.

—In a Gondola

'You have black eyes, Love—you are, sure enough,
My peerless bride—

—Pippa Passes

Through one's after-supper musings,
Some lost lady of old years
With her beauteous vain endeavour
And goodness unrepaid as ever;
The face, accustomed to refusings

—Waring

Escape me?
Never–
Beloved!
While I am I, and you are you,
So long as the world contains us both,
Me the loving and you the loth,
While the one eludes, must the other pursue.

—*Life in a Love*

If you say, "you love him"—straight, "he'll not be gulled!"

—*Pippa Passes*

You'll love me yet!—and I can tarry
Your love's protracted growing:
June reared that bunch of flowers you carry,
From seeds of April's sowing.

I plant a heartful now: some seed
At least is sure to strike,
And yield–what you'll not pluck indeed,
Not love, but, may be, like.

You'll look at least on love's remains,
A grave's one violet:
Your look?—that pays a thousand pains.
What's death? You'll love me yet!

—*Pippa Passes*

Therefore to whom turn I but to thee, the ineffable Name?

—*Abt Vogler*

Thou art my single day

—In Three Days

Where I find her not, beauties vanish;
Whither I follow her, beauties flee;
Is there no method to tell her in Spanish
June's twice June since she breathed it with me?
Come, bud, show me the least of her traces,
Treasure my lady's lightest footfall!
—Ah, you may flout and turn up your faces—
Roses, you are not so fair after all!

—Garden Fancies

Could thought of mine improve you?

—In a Gondola

Doubt you whether
This she felt as, looking at me,
Mine and her souls rushed together?

—Cristina

And I ventured to remind her,
I suppose with a voice of less steadiness
Than usual, for my feeling exceeded me,
—Something to the effect that I was in readiness
Whenever God should please she needed me

—The Flight of the Duchess

Oh, Angel of the East, one, one gold look
Across the waters to this twilight nook

—Rudel to the Lady of Tripoli

Robert Browning on Love

And "love"
Is a short word that says so very much!

—A Blot In the 'Scutcheon

❧

Strangers like you that pictured countenance,
The depth and passion of its earnest glance

—My Last Duchess

❧

Heap Cassia, sandal-buds and stripes
Of labdanum, and aloe-balls,
Smeared with dull nard an Indian wipes
From out her hair: such balsam falls

—Heap Cassia, Sandal-Buds and Stripes

❧

Let my hands frame your face in your hair's gold

—Andrea del Sarto

"Is it true,"
Thou'lt ask, "some eyes are beautiful and new?
"Some hair,—how can one choose but grasp such
wealth?
"And if a man would press his lips to lips
"Fresh as the wilding hedge-rose-cup there slips
"The dew-drop out of, must it be by stealth?

—Any Wife to Any Husband

Is it not in my nature to adore…?

—Pauline

God bless in turn
That heart which beats, those eyes which mildly burn
With love for all men! I, to-night at least,
Would be that holy and beloved priest.

—Pippa Passes

The heroic in passion, or in action,—
Or, lowered for sense's satisfaction,
To the mere outside of human creatures,
Mere perfect form and faultless features.

—*Christmas-Eve and Easter-Day*

You creature with the eyes!
If I could look forever up to them,
As now you let me—I believe all sin,
All memory of wrong done, suffering borne,
Would drop down, low and lower, to the earth
Whence all that's low comes, and there touch and stay
—Never to overtake the rest of me,
All that, unspotted, reaches up to you,
Drawn by those eyes!

—*Pippa Passes*

The year's at the spring,
And day's at the morn;
Morning's at seven;
The hill-side's dew-pearled;
The lark's on the wing,
The snail's on the thorn;
God's in his Heaven—
All's right with the world!

—*Pippa Passes*

Was a lady such a lady, cheeks so round
and lips so red,—
On her neck the small face buoyant, like
a bell-flower on its bed,
O'er the breast's superb abundance where
a man might base his head?

—*A Toccata of Galuppi's*

So, we leave the sweet face fondly there:
　　Be its beauty
　　Its sole duty!

—A Pretty Woman

Witchcraft's a fault in him,
　　For you're bewitched.

—A Blot In the 'Scutcheon

'Tis the weakness in strength, that I cry for! my flesh,
　　that I seek

—Saul

How shall I fix you, fire you, freeze you,
Break my heart at your feet to please you?
Oh, to possess and be possessed!
Hearts that beat 'neath each pallid breast!
Once but of love, the poesy, the passion,
Drink but once and die!—In vain, the same fashion

—*Women and Roses*

—Love, with Greece and Rome in ken,
Bade her scribes abhor the trick
Of poetry and rhetoric,
And exult with hearts set free,
In blessed imbecility

—*Christmas-Eve and Easter-Day*

Love's Hope

What spell or what charm…?

—*Saul*

A novel grace and a beauty strange.

—*Women and Roses*

Your love can claim no right
O'er her save pure love's claim

—*A Blot In the 'Scutcheon*

She does not also take it for earnest, I hope?

—*Pippa Passes*

Then,—if my heart's strength serve,
And through all and each
Of the veils I reach
To her soul and never swerve,
Knitting an iron nerve—
Command her soul to advance
And inform the shape
Which has made escape
And before my countenance
Answers me glance for glance—

—Mesmerism

On the face alone he expends his devotion

—Christmas-Eve and Easter-Day

There's a woman like a dew-drop, she's so purer than
the purest;
And her noble heart's the noblest, yes, and her sure
faith's the surest:
And her eyes are dark and humid, like the depth on
depth of lustre
Hid i' the harebell, while her tresses, sunnier than the
wild-grape cluster,
Gush in golden-tinted plenty down her neck's rose-
misted marble:
Then her voice's music . . . call it the well's bubbling,
the bird's warble!

—*A Blot In the 'Scutcheon*

If one could have that little head of hers
Painted upon a background of pure gold

—*A Face*

I had devised a certain tale
Which, when 'twas told her, could not fail
Persuade a peasant of its truth;

—The Italian In England

"Speak, I love thee best!"
He exclaimed:
"Let thy love my own foretell!"
I confessed:
"Clasp my heart on thine
"Now unblamed,
"Since upon thy soul as well
"Hangeth mine!"

—In a Year

When I do come, she will speak not, she will stand,
Either hand
On my shoulder, give her eyes the first embrace
Of my face,
Ere we rush, ere we extinguish sight and speech
Each on each.

—Love Among the Ruins

Love's Hope

I believe
If once I threw my arms about your neck
And sunk my head upon your breast, that I
Should weep again.

—A Blot In the 'Scutcheon

As I ride, as I ride,
Could I loose what Fate has tied,
Ere I pried, she should hide
(As I ride, as I ride)
All that's meant me—satisfied
When the Prophet and the Bride
Stop veins I'd have subside
As I ride, as I ride!

—Through the Metidja to Abd-El-Kadr

Here's my case. Of old I used to love him.
This same unseen friend, before I knew:
Dream there was none like him, none above him,—
Wake to hope and trust my dream was true.

—Fears and Scruples

Robert Browning on Love

I wonder do you feel to-day
As I have felt since, hand in hand,
We sat down on the grass, to stray
In spirit better through the land,
This morn of Rome and May?

For me, I touched a thought, I know,
Has tantalized me many times,
(Like turns of thread the spiders throw
Mocking across our path) for rhymes
To catch at and let go.

Help me to hold it! First it left
The yellowing fennel, run to seed
There, branching from the brickwork's cleft,
Some old tomb's ruin: yonder weed
Took up the floating weft,

Where one small orange cup amassed
Five beetles,—blind and green they grope
Among the honey-meal: and last,
Everywhere on the grassy slope
I traced it. Hold it fast!

The champaign with its endless fleece
Of feathery grasses everywhere!
Silence and passion, joy and peace,
An everlasting wash of air—
Rome's ghost since her decease.

Love's Hope

Such life here, through such lengths of hours,
Such miracles performed in play,
Such primal naked forms of flowers,
Such letting nature have her way
While heaven looks from its towers!

How say you? Let us, O my dove,
Let us be unashamed of soul,
As earth lies bare to heaven above!
How is it under our control
To love or not to love?

I would that you were all to me,
You that are just so much, no more.
Nor yours nor mine—nor slave nor free!
Where does the fault lie? What the core
O' the wound, since wound must be?

I would I could adopt your will,
See with your eyes, and set my heart
Beating by yours, and drink my fill
At your soul's springs,—your part my part
In life, for good and ill.

No. I yearn upward, touch you close,
Then stand away. I kiss your cheek,
Catch your soul's warmth,—I pluck the rose
And love it more than tongue can speak—
Then the good minute goes.

Already how am I so far
Out of that minute? Must I go
Still like the thistle-ball, no bar,
Onward, whenever light winds blow,
Fixed by no friendly star?

Just when I seemed about to learn!
Where is the thread now? Off again!
The old trick! Only I discern—
Infinite passion, and the pain
Of finite hearts that yearn.

—Two in the Campagna

Yet so we look ere we will love; not I

—Pippa Passes

Truth is within ourselves.

—Paracelsus

Too bold, too confident she'll still face down
The spitefullest of talkers in our town.

—In Three Days

And you—O, how feel you? Feel you for me?

—Pippa Passes

Grow old along with me!
The best is yet to be,
The last of life, for which the first was made:
Our times are in His hand
Who saith 'A whole I planned,
Youth shows but half; trust God: see all, nor be
afraid!'

—Rabbi Ben Ezra

Shall I sonnet-sing you about myself?
Do I live in a house you would like to see?
Is it scant of gear, has it store of pelf?
"Unlock my heart with a sonnet-key?"

—*House*

I said—Then, dearest, since 'tis so,
Since now at length my fate I know,
Since nothing all my love avails,
Since all, my life seemed meant for, fails,
Since this was written and needs must be—
My whole heart rises up to bless
Your name in pride and thankfulness!
Take back the hope you gave,—I claim
—Only a memory of the same,
—And this beside, if you will not blame,
Your leave for one more last ride with me.

—*The Last Ride Together*

Love's Hope

Ages ago, a lady there,
At the farthest window facing the East,
Asked, "Who rides by with the royal air?"

The bridesmaids' prattle around her ceased;
She leaned forth, one on either hand;
They saw how the blush of the bride increased—

They felt by its beats her heart expand—
As one at each ear and both in a breath
Whispered, "The Great-Duke Ferdinand."

—*The Statue and the Bust*

***

So, I shall see her in three days
And just one night, but nights are short,
Then two long hours, and that is morn.
See how I come, unchanged, unworn!
Feel, where my life broke off from thine,
How fresh the splinters keep and fine,—
Only a touch and we combine!

—*In Three Days*

Now, stay ever as thou art!

—*In a Gondola*

Worth how well, those dark grey eyes,
That hair so dark and dear, how worth
That a man should strive and agonize,
And taste a veriest hell on earth
For the hope of such a prize!

—*By the Fire-Side*

And thus we sit together now,
And all night long we have not stirred,
And yet God has not said a word!

—*Porphyria's Lover*

Love's Hope

Love, we are in God's hand.

—*Andrea del Sarto*

And yet thou art the nobler of us two

—*Any Wife to Any Husband*

You turn your face, but does it bring your heart?

—*Andrea del Sarto*

You might have turned and tried a man,
Set him a space to weary and wear,
And prove which suited more your plan,
His best of hope or his worst despair,
Yet end as he began.

—*By the Fire-Side*

I can simply wish I might refute you,
Wish my friend would,—by a word, a wink,—
Bid me stop that foolish mouth,—you brute you!
He keeps absent,—why, I cannot think.

—Fears and Scruples

Saith, he knoweth but one thing,—what he knows?
That God is good and the rest is breath;
Why else is the same styled Sharon's rose?
Once a rose, ever a rose, he saith.

—The Heretic's Tragedy

All's our own, to make the most of, Sweet—
Sing and say for,
Watch and pray for,
Keep a secret or go boast of, Sweet!

—A Pretty Woman

Love's Hope

My love, this is the bitterest, that thou—
Who art all truth, and who dost love me now
As thine eyes say, as thy voice breaks to say—
Shouldst love so truly, and couldst love me still

—Any Wife to Any Husband

⸎

Where the apple reddens
Never pry—
Lest we lose our Edens,
Eve and I.

—A Woman's Last Word

⸎

See, how she looks now, dressed
In a sledging-cap and vest!
'Tis a huge fur cloak—
Like a reindeer's yoke
Falls the lappet along the breast:
Sleeves for her arms to rest,
Or to hang, as my Love likes best.

—A Lovers' Quarrel

An hour, and she returned alone
Exactly where my glove was thrown.

—The Italian In England

The peasants from the village go
To work among the maize; you know,
With us in Lombardy, they bring
Provisions packed on mules, a string
With little bells that cheer their task,
And casks, and boughs on every cask
To keep the sun's heat from the wine;
These I let pass in jingling line,
And, close on them, dear noisy crew,
The peasants from the village, too;
For at the very rear would troop
Their wives and sisters in a group
To help, I knew. When these had passed,
I threw my glove to strike the last,
Taking the chance: she did not start,
Much less cry out, but stooped apart,
One instant rapidly glanced round,
And saw me beckon from the ground.
A wild bush grows and hides my crypt;
She picked my glove up while she stripped
A branch off, then rejoined the rest
With that; my glove lay in her breast.

—The Italian In England

What should your chamber do?
—With all its rarities that ache
In silence while day lasts, but wake
At night-time and their life renew,
Suspended just to pleasure you

—In a Gondola

And yet—she has not spoke so long!
What if heaven be that, fair and strong
At life's best, with our eyes upturned
Whither life's flower is first discerned,
We, fixed so, ever should so abide?
What if we still ride on, we two
With life for ever old yet new

—The Last Ride Together

As still he envied me, so fair she was!

—The Bishop Orders His Tomb

She turned on her side and slept. Just so!
So we resolve on a thing and sleep:
So did the lady, ages ago.

—The Statue and the Bust

Have you found your life distasteful?
My life did and does smack sweet.
Was your youth of pleasure wasteful?
Mine I saved and hold complete.
Do your joys with age diminish?
When mine fail me, I'll complain.
Must in death your daylight finish?
My sun sets to rise again.

—At the "Mermaid"

Tell me, as lovers should, heart-free,
Something to prove his love of me.

—The Confessional

You like us for a glance, you know–
For a word's sake

—A Pretty Woman

Would I suffer for him that I love?

—Saul

All the breath and the bloom of the year in the bag of
one bee:
All the wonder and wealth of the mine in the heart of
one gem:
In the core of one pearl all the shade and the shine of
the sea:
Breath and bloom, shade and shine,—wonder, wealth,
and—how far above them—
Truth, that's brighter than gem,
Trust, that's purer than pearl,—
Brightest truth, purest trust in the universe—all were
for me
In the kiss of one girl.

—Summum Bonum

As thy Love is discovered almighty, almighty be
proved
Thy power, that exists with and for it, of being
Beloved!

—*Saul*

All I believed is true!
I am able yet
All I want, to get
By a method as strange as new:
Dare I trust the same to you?

—*Mesmerism*

Oh, to love less what one has injured! Dove,
Whose pinion I have rashly hurt, my breast—
Shall my heart's warmth not nurse thee into strength?
Flower I have crushed, shall I not care for thee?

—*A Blot In the 'Scutcheon*

Love's
Promise

If I gave him what he praised
Was it strange?

—*In a Year*

That is it.
Our happiness would, as you say, exceed
The whole world's best of blisses

—*A Blot In the 'Scutcheon*

I send my heart up to thee, all my heart
In this my singing.
For the stars help me, and the sea bears part;
The very night is clinging
Closer to Venice' streets to leave one space
Above me, whence thy face
May light my joyous heart to thee its dwelling-place.

—*In a Gondola*

Oh, the beautiful girl, too white,
Who lived at Pornic, down by the sea,
Just where the sea and the Loire unite!
And a boasted name in Brittany
She bore, which I will not write.

Too white, for the flower of life is red:
Her flesh was the soft seraphic screen
Of a soul that is meant (her parents said)
To just see earth, and hardly be seen,
And blossom in heaven instead.

Yet earth saw one thing, one how fair!
One grace that grew to its full on earth:
Smiles might be sparse on her cheek so spare,
And her waist want half a girdle's girth,
But she had her great gold hair.

Hair, such a wonder of flix and floss,
Freshness and fragrance—floods of it, too!
Gold, did I say? Nay, gold's mere dross: Here,
Life smiled, "Think what I meant to do!"
And Love sighed, "Fancy my loss!"

So, when she died, it was scarce more strange
Than that, when delicate evening dies,
And you follow its spent sun's pallid range,
There's a shoot of colour startles the skies
With sudden, violent change,—

That, while the breath was nearly to seek,
As they put the little cross to her lips,
She changed; a spot came out on her cheek,
A spark from her eye in mid-eclipse,
And she broke forth, "I must speak!"

—*Gold Hair*

I scarce grieve o'er
The past. We'll love on; you will love me still.

—*A Blot In the 'Scutcheon*

First I will pray. Do Thou
That ownest the soul,
Yet wilt grant control
To another, nor disallow
For a time, restrain me now!
I admonish me while I may,
Not to squander guilt,
Since require Thou wilt
At my hand its price one day
What the price is, who can say?

—*Mesmerism*

The grey sea and the long black land;
And the yellow half-moon large and low;
And the startled little waves that leap
In fiery ringlets from their sleep,
As I gain the cove with pushing prow,
And quench its speed i' the slushy sand.
Then a mile of warm sea-scented beach;
Three fields to cross till a farm appears;
A tap at the pane, the quick sharp scratch
And blue spurt of a lighted match,
And a voice less loud, thro' its joys and fears,
Than the two hearts beating each to each!

—Meeting at Night

Come what, come will,
You have been happy: take my hand!

—A Blot In the 'Scutcheon

I need thee still and might miss perchance.
Today is not wholly lost, beside,
With its hope of my lady's countenance

—The Statue and the Bust

You smile? why, there's my picture ready made

—*Andrea del Sarto*

For spring bade the sparrows pair,
And the boys and girls gave guesses

—*Youth and Art*

How else should love's perfected noontide follow?
All the dawn promised shall the day perform.

—*A Blot In the 'Scutcheon*

I believe in you, but that's not enough:
Give my conviction a clinch!

—*Master Hugues of Saxe-Gotha*

And my eyes hold her! What is worth
The rest of heaven, the rest of earth?

—*In Three Days*

Love's Promise

One day as the lady saw her youth
Depart, and the silver thread that streaked
Her hair, and, worn by the serpent's tooth,

The brow so puckered, the chin so peaked,—
And wondered who the woman was,
Hollow-eyed and haggard-cheeked,

Fronting her silent in the glass—
"Summon here," she suddenly said,
"Before the rest of my old self pass."

—The Statue and the Bust

Through the Valley of Love I went,
In the lovingest spot to abide,
And just on the verge where I pitched my tent,
I found Hate dwelling beside.
And further, I traversed Hate's grove,
In the hatefullest nook to dwell;
But lo, where I flung myself prone, couched Love
Where the shadow threefold fell.

—Pippa Passes

Never the time and the place
And the loved one all together!
This path–how soft to pace!
This May–what magic weather!
Where is the loved one's face?
In a dream that loved one's face meets mine,
But the house is narrow, the place is bleak
Where, outside, rain and wind combine
With a furtive ear, if I strive to speak,
With a hostile eye at my flushing cheek,
With a malice that marks each word, each sign!
O enemy sly and serpentine,
Uncoil thee from the waking man!
Do I hold the Past
Thus firm and fast
Yet doubt if the Future hold I can?
This path so soft to pace shall lead
Through the magic of May to herself indeed!
Or narrow if needs the house must be,
Outside are the storms and strangers; we—
Oh, close, safe, warm sleep I and she
—I and she!

—*Never the Time and the Place*

Can I forgo the trust that he loves me?

—*Pauline*

❦

Fail I alone, in words and deeds?
Why, all men strive and who succeeds?

—*The Last Ride Together*

❦

I have but to be by thee, and thy hand
Will never let mine go, nor heart withstand
The beating of my heart to reach its place.
When shall I look for thee and feel thee gone?
When cry for the old comfort and find none?
Never, I know! Thy soul is in thy face.

—*Any Wife to Any Husband*

So, the year's done with
(Love me for ever!)
All March begun with,
April's endeavour;
May-wreaths that bound me
June needs must sever;
Now snows fall round me,
Quenching June's fever—
(Love me for ever!)

—Earth's Immortalities

I shall never, in the years remaining,
Paint you pictures, no, nor carve you statues.
Make you music that should all-express me;
So it seems; I stand on my attainment.
This of verse alone, one life allows me;
Verse and nothing else have I to give you;
Other heights in other lives, God willing;
All the gifts from all the heights, your own, Love.

—One Word More

Love was the startling thing, the new:
Love was the all-sufficient too;
And seeing that, you see the rest:
As a babe can find its mother's breast
As well in darkness as in light,
Love shut our eyes, and all seemed right.

—Christmas-Eve and Easter-Day

There they are, my fifty men and women
Naming me the fifty poems finished!
Take them, Love, the book and me together;
Where the heart lies, let the brain lie also.

—One Word More

Henceforth be loved as heart can love

—The Flight of the Duchess

Think, when our one soul understands
The great Word which makes all things new,
When earth breaks up and heaven expands,
How will the change strike me and you
In the house not made with hands?

—By the Fire-Side

Shall our lip with the honey be bright?

—Saul

I shall see her in three days
And one night, now the nights are short

—In Three Days

And never the King told the story,
How bringing a glove brought such glory,
But the wife smiled—"His nerves are grown firmer:
"Mine he brings now and utters no murmur."

—The Glove

How forget the thrill
Thro' and thro' me as I thought, 'The gladlier
Lives my friend because I love him still!'

—Fears and Scruples

Then we would up and pace,
For a change, about the place,
Each with arm o'er neck:
'Tis our quarter-deck,
We are seamen in woeful case.
Help in the ocean-space!
Or, if no help, we'll embrace.

—A Lovers' Quarrel

My God, my God! let me for once look on thee
As tho' nought else existed: we alone.
And as creation crumbles, my soul's spark
Expands till I can say, 'Even from myself
I need thee, and I feel thee, and I love thee;
I do not plead my rapture in thy works
For love of thee—or that I feel as one
Who cannot die—but there is that in me
Which turns to thee, which loves, or which should
love.'

—Pauline

In a minute can lovers exchange a word?
If a word did pass, which I do not think,
Only one out of the thousand heard.

—The Statue and the Bust

Close on her heels, the dingy satins
Of a female something past me flitted,
With lips as much too white, as a streak
Lay far too red on each hollow cheek;
And it seemed the very door-hinge pitied
All that was left of a woman once

—Christmas-Eve and Easter-Day

Hardly shall I tell my joys and sorrows,
Hopes and fears, belief and disbelieving:
I am mine and yours

—One Word More

I would give thee new life altogether, as good, ages
hence,
As this moment,—had love but the warrant, love's
heart to dispense!

—Saul

The sentence no sooner was uttered,
Than over the rails a glove flattered.

—*The Glove*

Mark him, Austin; that's true love!
Ours must begin again.

—*A Blot In the 'Scutcheon*

And I know, while thus the quiet-coloured eve
Smiles to leave
To their folding, all our many-tinkling fleece
In such peace,
And the slopes and rills in undistinguished grey
Melt away—
That a girl with eager eyes and yellow hair
Waits me there
In the turret whence the charioteers caught soul
For the goal,
When the king looked, where she looks now,
breathless, dumb
Till I come.

Of the life he was gifted and filled with? to make such
a soul,
Such a body, and then such an earth for insphering
the whole?

—Saul

See the creature stalking
While we speak!
Hush and hide the talking,
Cheek on cheek!

—A Woman's Last Word

Thou shalt love and be loved by, for ever: a Hand like
this hand
Shall throw open the gates of new life to thee!

—Saul

There is no god in life by love—but love!
What else looks good is some shade flung from love;
Love gilds it, gives it worth.

—In a Balcony

Her beauty is not strange to you, it seems—
You cannot know the good and tender heart,
Its girl's trust and its woman's constancy,
How pure yet passionate, how calm yet kind,
How grave yet joyous, how reserved yet free

—A Blot In the 'Scutcheon

Ecstasy of Love

Ecstasy of Love

Have and hold, then and there,
Her, from head to foot,
Breathing and mute,
Passive and yet aware,
In the grasp of my steady stare—

Hold and have, there and then,
All her body and soul
That completes my whole,
All that women add to men,
In the clutch of my steady ken—
Having and holding, till
I imprint her fast
On the void at last

—Mesmerism

* * *

Yet now my heart leaps, O beloved!

—Saul

65

You and I would rather see that angel,
Painted by the tenderness of Dante,
Would we not?–than read a fresh Inferno.

—One Word More

❧

Face to face the lovers stood
A single minute and no more,
While the bridegroom bent as a man subdued —

—The Statue and the Bust

❧

I catch your meaning now,
And I obey you! Hist! This tree will serve.

—A Blot In the 'Scutcheon

Ecstasy of Love

So will I bury me while burning,
Quench like him at a plunge my yearning,
Eyes in your eyes, lips on your lips!
Fold me fast where the cincture slips,
Prison all my soul in eternities of pleasure

—*Women and Roses*

Then I reach, I must believe,
Not her soul in vain,
For to me again
It reaches, and past retrieve
Is wound in the toils I weave;

And must follow as I require,
As befits a thrall,
Bringing flesh and all,
Essence and earth-attire,
To the source of the tractile fire:

Till the house called hers, not mine,
With a growing weight
Seems to suffocate
If she break not its leaden line
And escape from its close confine.

—*Mesmerism*

I know, sir, it's improper,
My poor mind's out of tune.

—*Confessions*

⁂

Such am I: the secret's mine now!
She has lost me, I have gained her

—*Cristina*

⁂

Man I am and man would be, Love—merest man and
nothing more.
Bid me seem no other! Eagles boast of pinions—let
them soar!
I may put forth angel's plumage, once unmanned, but
not before.

Now on earth to stand suffices,—nay, if kneeling
serves, to kneel:
Here you front me, here I find the all of heaven that
earth can feel:
Sense looks straight,—not over, under,—perfect sees
beyond appeal.

Ecstasy of Love

Good you are and wise, full circle: what to me were
more outside?
Wiser wisdom, better goodness? Ah, such want the
angel's wide
Sense to take and hold and keep them! Mine at least
has never tried.

—Ferishtah's Fancies

He looked at her, as a lover can;
She looked at him, as one who awakes:
The past was a sleep, and their life began.

—The Statue and the Bust

So, she'd efface the score,
And forgive me as before.
It is twelve o'clock:
I shall hear her knock

In the worst of a storm's uproar,
I shall pull her through the door,
I shall have her for evermore!

—A Lovers' Quarrel

Like the doors of a casket-shrine,
See, on either side,
Her two arms divide
Till the heart betwixt makes sign,
Take me, for I am thine!

"Now—now"—the door is heard!
Hark, the stairs! and near—
Nearer—and here—
"Now!" and at call the third
She enters without a word.

On doth she march and on
To the fancied shape;
It is, past escape,
Herself, now: the dream is done
And the shadow and she are one.

—*Mesmerism*

What of soul was left, I wonder, when the kissing had
to stop?

—*A Toccata of Galuppi's*

Where is the use of the lip's red charm,
The heaven of hair, the pride of the brow,
And the blood that blues the inside arm—

—The Statue and the Bust

❦

Out of your whole life give but a moment!
All of your life that has gone before,
All to come after it,—so you ignore,
So you make perfect the present,—condense,
In a rapture of rage, for perfection's endowment,
Thought and feeling and soul and sense—
Merged in a moment which gives me at last
You around me for once, you beneath me,
above me—
Me—sure that, despite of time future, time past,—
This tick of life-time's one moment you love me!
How long such suspension may linger? Ah, Sweet,—
The moment eternal—just that and no more—
When ecstasy's utmost we clutch at the core,
While cheeks burn, arms open, eyes shut, and lips
meet!

—Now

Do lovers in romances sin that way?

—*Pippa Passes*

Oh heart! oh blood that freezes, blood that burns!
Earth's returns
For whole centuries of folly, noise and sin!
Shut them in,
With their triumphs and their glories and the rest!
Love is best.

—*Love Among the Ruins*

Did young people take their pleasure when the sea
was warm in May?
Balls and masks begun at midnight, burning ever to
mid-day,
When they made up fresh adventures for the morrow,
do you say?

Was a lady such a lady, cheeks so round and lips so
red—
On her neck the small face buoyant, like a bell-flower
on its bed,
O'er the breast's superb abundance where a man
might base his head?

Well, and it was graceful of them—they'd break talk
off and afford
—She, to bite her mask's black velvet—he, to finger
on his sword,
While you sat and played Toccatas, stately at the
clavichord?

What? Those lesser thirds so plaintive, sixths
diminished, sigh on sigh,
Told them something? Those suspensions, those
solutions–"Must we die?"
Those commiserating sevenths—"Life might last! we
can but try!"

"Were you happy?"—"Yes."—"And are you still as
happy?"—"Yes. And you?"
—"Then, more kisses!"—"Did *I* stop them, when a
million seemed so few?"
Hark, the dominant's persistence till it must be
answered to!

—*A Toccata of Galuppi's*

Since first I noted
All this, I've groaned as if a fiery net
Plucked me this way and that—fire if I turned
To her, fire if I turned to you, and fire
If down I flung myself and strove to die.

—A Blot In the 'Scutcheon

Breathe but one breath
Rose-beauty above,
And all that was death
Grows life, grows love,
Grows love!

—Wanting Is—What?

O lyric Love, half angel and half bird
And all a wonder and a wild desire,—

—The Ring and the Book

For, there! have I drawn or no
Life to that lip?
Do my fingers dip
In a flame which again they throw
On the cheek that breaks a-glow?

—*Mesmerism*

Yet my passion must wait a night, nor cool —
For tonight the Envoy arrives from France
Whose heart I unlock with thyself, my tool.

—*The Statue and the Bust*

This body had no soul before, but slept
Or stirred, was beauteous or ungainly, free

—*Pippa Passes*

Her cheek once more
Blushed bright beneath my burning kiss

—*Porphyria's Lover*

❧

They trail me, these three godless knaves,
Past every church that saints and saves,
Nor stop till, where the cold sea raves
By Lido's wet accursed graves,
They scoop mine, roll me to its brink,
And . . . on thy breast I sink

—*In a Gondola*

❧

Burn upward each to his point of bliss—
Since, the end of life being manifest,
He had burned his way through the world to this.

—*The Statue and the Bust*

You should not take a fellow eight years old
And make him swear to never kiss the girls.

—Fra Lippo Lippi

I am queen of thee, floweret!
And each fleshy blossom
Preserve I not—(safer
Than leaves that embower it,
Or shells that embosom)—
From weevil and chafer?
Laugh through my pane then; solicit the bee;
Gibe him, be sure; and, in midst of thy glee,
Love thy queen, worship me!

—Pippa Passes

O my love, my all, my one!

—A Serenade at the Villa

So free we seem, so fettered fast we are!

—Andrea del Sarto

So, I gave her eyes my own eyes to take,
My hand sought hers as in earnest need,
And round she turned for my noble sake,
And gave me herself indeed.

—A Light Woman

Oh, what a fancy ecstatic
Was the poor heart's, ere the wanderer went on—
Love to be saved for it, proffered to, spent on!

—Misconceptions

What a thing friendship is, world without end!

—The Flight of the Duchess

Ecstasy of Love

Speak to me—not of me.

—Pippa Passes

Till I felt where the foldskirts fly open. Then once
more I prayed,
And opened the foldskirts and entered, and was not
afraid

—Saul

Out of doors into the night!
On to the maze
Of the wild wood-ways,
Not turning to left nor right
From the pathway, blind with sight—

Making thro' rain and wind
O'er the broken shrubs,
'Twixt the stems and stubs,
With a still, composed, strong mind,
Nor a care for the world behind—

Swifter and still more swift,
As the crowding peace
Doth to joy increase
In the wide blind eyes uplift
Thro' the darkness and the drift!

While I—to the shape, I too
Feel my soul dilate
Nor a whit abate,
And relax not a gesture due,
As I see my belief come true.

—Mesmerism

Heart to heart
And lips to lips! Yet once more, ere we part,
Clasp me and make me thine, as mine thou art!

—In a Gondola

Well, dear, in-doors with you!

—Another Way of Love

Till God's own smile came out:
That was thy face!

—*Apparitions*

I follow wherever I am led,
Knowing so well the leader's hand:
Oh woman-country, wooed not wed,
Loved all the more by earth's male-lands,
Laid to their hearts instead!

—*By the Fire-Side*

Your soft hand is a woman of itself

—*Andrea del Sarto*

And . . . is it thou I feel?

—*In a Gondola*

But above night too, like only the next,
The second of a wondrous sequence,
Reaching in rare and rarer frequence,
Till the heaven of heavens were circumflexed,
Another rainbow rose, a mightier,
Fainter, flushier and flightier,—
Rapture dying along its verge.
Oh, whose foot shall I see emerge,
Whose, from the straining topmost dark,
On to the keystone of that arc?

—*Christmas-Eve and Easter-Day*

Be a god and hold me
With a charm!
Be a man and fold me
With thine arm!

—*A Woman's Last Word*

My last thought was at least not vain:
I and my mistress, side by side
Shall be together, breathe and ride,
So, one day more am I deified.
Who knows but the world may end tonight?

—The Last Ride Together

He will but press the closer, breathe more warm
Against her cheek; how should she mind the storm?

—Pippa Passes

Love so, then, if thou wilt! Give all thou canst

—Any Wife to Any Husband

Round the cape of a sudden came the sea,
And the sun looked over the mountain's rim:
And straight was a path of gold for him,
And the need of a world of men for me.

—Parting at Morning

How good is man's life, the mere living!

—Saul

The moth's kiss, first!
Kiss me as if you made believe
You were not sure, this eve,
How my face, your flower, had pursed
Its petals up; so, here and there
You brush it, till I grow aware
Who wants me, and wide ope I burst.

—In a Gondola

"Wilt thou fall at the very last
"Breathless, half in trance
"With the thrill of the great deliverance,
"Into our arms for evermore;
"And thou shalt know, those arms once curled
"About thee, what we knew before,
"How love is the only good in the world.

—*The Flight of the Duchess*

You heard music; that was I.

—*A Serenade at the Villa*

I had wealth and ease,
Beauty, youth:
Since my lover gave me love,
I gave these.

—*In a Year*

I listened with heart fit to break.
When glided in Porphyria; straight
She shut the cold out and the storm,
And kneeled and made the cheerless grate
Blaze up, and all the cottage warm

—*Porphyria's Lover*

To grasp her–(divers who pick pearls so grope)

—*Pan and Luna*

It was ordained to be so, sweet!—and best
Comes now, beneath thine eyes, upon thy breast.
Still kiss me!

—*In a Gondola*

That's the wise thrush; he sings each song twice over,
Lest you should think he never could recapture
The first fine careless rapture!

—Home Thoughts from Abroad

Teach me, only teach, Love
As I ought
I will speak thy speech, Love,
Think thy thought—

—A Woman's Last Word

Love, if you knew the light
That your soul casts in my sight,
How I look to you
For the pure and true
And the beauteous and the right

—A Lovers' Quarrel

By the pain-throb, triumphantly winning intensified
bliss

—*Saul*

"This woman's heart and soul and brain
"Are mine as much as this gold chain
"She bids me wear; which" (say again)
"I choose to make by cherishing
"A precious thing, or choose to fling
"Over the boat-side, ring by ring."

—*In a Gondola*

Nay but you, who do not love her,
Is she not pure gold, my mistress?
Holds earth aught—speak truth—above her?
Aught like this tress, see, and this tress,
And this last fairest tress of all,
So fair, see, ere I let it fall?

Ecstasy of Love

Because, you spend your lives in praising;
To praise, you search the wide world over:
Then why not witness, calmly gazing,
If earth holds aught—speak truth—above her?
Above this tress, and this, I touch
But cannot praise, I love so much!

—Song

I am knit round
As with a charm, by sin and lust and pride

—Pauline

And she,—she lies in my hand as tame
As a pear late basking over a wall;
Just a touch to try and off it came;
'Tis mine,—can I let it fall?

—A Light Woman

And I shall behold thee, face to face

—*Christmas-Eve and Easter-Day*

I've a Friend, over the sea;
I like him, but he loves me.

And I've a Lady—there he wakes,
The laughing fiend and prince of snakes
Within me, at her name, to pray
Fate send some creature in the way
Of my love for her, to be down-torn,
Upthrust and outward-borne,
So I might prove myself that sea
Of passion which I needs must be!
Call my thoughts false and my fancies quaint
And my style infirm and its figures faint,
All the critics say, and more blame yet,
And not one angry word you get.
But, please you, wonder I would put
My cheek beneath that lady's foot
Rather than trample under mine
The laurels of the Florentine,
And you shall see how the devil spends
A fire God gave for other ends!
I tell you, I stride up and down
This garret, crowned with love's best crown,
And feasted with love's perfect feast,
To think I kill for her, at least,

Body and soul and peace and fame,
Alike youth's end and manhood's aim,
—So is my spirit, as flesh with sin,
Filled full, eaten out and in
With the face of her, the eyes of her,
The lips, the little chin, the stir
Of shadow round her mouth; and she
—I'll tell you,—calmly would decree
That I should roast at a slow fire,
If that would compass her desire

—*Time's Revenges*

Hold on, hope hard in the subtle thing
That's spirit: tho' cloistered fast, soar free

—*A Wall*

Robert Browning on Love

The bee's kiss, now!
Kiss me as if you entered gay
My heart at some noonday,
A bud that dares not disallow
The claim, so all is rendered up,
And passively its shattered cup
Over your head to sleep I bow.

—In a Gondola

But you sink, for your eyes
Are altering—altered! Stay—"I love you, love" . . .
I could prevent it if I understood:
More of your words to me; was't in the tone
Or the words, your power?

—Pippa Passes

Now, what is it makes pulsate the robe?
Why tremble the sprays? What life o'erbrims
The body,—the house no eye can probe,—
Divined, as beneath a robe, the limbs?

—A Wall

That moment she was mine, mine, fair

—Porphyria's Lover

O loaded curls, release your store
Of warmth and scent, as once before
The tingling hair did, lights and darks
Outbreaking into fairy sparks

—In Three Days

I, still with a gesture fit
Of my hands that best
Do my soul's behest,
Pointing the power from it,
While myself do steadfast sit—
Steadfast and still the same
On my object bent,
While the hands give vent
To my ardour and my aim
And break into very flame—

—Mesmerism

Since words are only words. Give o'er!

—In a Gondola

What—why is this?
That whitening cheek, those still dilating eyes!

—Pippa Passes

For pleasant is this flesh;
Our soul, in its rose-mesh

—*Rabbi Ben Ezra*

∗∗∗∗∗

I have his heart, you know;
I may dispose of it: I give it you!

—*A Blot In the 'Scutcheon*

Love's
Despair

Why, with beauty, needs there money be,
Love with liking?

—*A Pretty Woman*

He may not shame such tender love and stay.

—*Childe Roland to the Dark Tower Came*

And this woman says, "My days were sunless and my
nights were moonless,
Parched the pleasant April herbage, and the lark's
heart's outbreak tuneless,
If you loved me not!" And I who—(ah, for words of
flame!) adore her,
Who am mad to lay my spirit prostrate palpably before
her—

—*A Blot In the 'Scutcheon*

Go, my Love.

—*Andrea del Sarto*

Oh, what a dawn of day!
How the March sun feels like May!
All is blue again
After last night's rain,
And the South dries the hawthorn-spray.
Only, my Love's away!
I'd as lief that the blue were grey.

—*A Lovers' Quarrel*

And as she died so must we die ourselves,
And thence ye may perceive the world's a dream.

—*The Bishop Orders His Tomb*

Why, 'twas my very fear of you, my love
Of you—(what passion like a boy's for one
Like you?)—that ruined me! I dreamed of you—
You, all accomplished, courted everywhere,
The scholar and the gentleman. I burned
To knit myself to you: but I was young,
And your surpassing reputation kept me
So far aloof! Oh, wherefore all that love?
With less of love, my glorious yesterday
Of praise and gentlest words and kindest looks,
Had taken place perchance six months ago.
Even now, how happy we had been!

—*A Blot In the 'Scutcheon*

Oh to love so, be so loved, yet so mistaken!

—*Epilogue to Asolando*

Too weak, for all her heart's endeavour,
To set its struggling passion free
From pride, and vainer ties dissever,
And give herself to me for ever.
But passion sometimes would prevail,
Nor could to-night's gay feast restrain
A sudden thought of one so pale
For love of her, and all in vain

—*Porphyria's Lover*

"Paint
Must never hope to reproduce the faint
Half-flush that dies along her throat:" such stuff
Was courtesy, she thought, and cause enough
For calling up that spot of joy. She had
A heart—how shall I say?—too soon made glad,
Too easily impressed: she liked whate'er
She looked on, and her looks went everywhere.

—*My Last Duchess*

Love's Despair

This is not our last meeting?
One night more.
And then—think, then!

—A Blot In the 'Scutcheon

So far as our story approaches the end,
Which do you pity the most of us three?—
My friend, or the mistress of my friend
With her wanton eyes, or me?

—A Light Woman

Can't we touch these bubbles then
But they break?

—In a Year

Now it is done, I seem the vilest worm
That crawls, to have betrayed my lady.

—A Blot In the 'Scutcheon

Hither we walked then, side by side,
Arm in arm and cheek to cheek,
And still I questioned or replied,
While my heart, convulsed to really speak,
Lay choking in its pride.

—By the Fire-Side

Or else kiss away one's soul on her?
Your love-fancies!
–A sick man sees
Truer, when his hot eyes roll on her!

—A Pretty Woman

Never any more,
While I live,
Need I hope to see his face
As before.
Once his love grown chill,
Mine may strive:
Bitterly we re-embrace,
Single still.

—In a Year

He's gone. Oh, I'll believe him every word!
I was so young, I loved him so, I had
No mother, God forgot me, and I fell.

      —A Blot In the 'Scutcheon

Room after room,
I hunt the house through
We inhabit together.
Heart, fear nothing, for, heart, thou shalt find her—
Next time, herself!—not the trouble behind her
Left in the curtain, the couch's perfume!
As she brushed it, the cornice-wreath blossomed anew:
Yon looking-glass gleaned at the wave of her feather.

Yet the day wears,
And door succeeds door;
I try the fresh fortune—
Range the wide house from the wing to the centre.
Still the same chance! she goes out as I enter.
Spend my whole day in the quest,—who cares?
But 'tis twilight, you see,—with such suites to explore,
Such closets to search, such alcoves to importune!

      —Love in a Life

You love him still, then?

—*A Blot In the 'Scutcheon*

So I grew wise in Love and Hate,
From simple that I was of late.
Once when I loved, I would enlace
Breast, eyelids, hands, feet, form and face
Of her I loved, in one embrace—
As if by mere love I could love immensely!
Once, when I hated, I would plunge
My sword, and wipe with the first lunge
My foe's whole life out like a sponge—
As if by mere hate I could hate intensely!
But now I am wiser, know better the fashion
How passion seeks aid from its opposite passion:
And if I see cause to love more, hate more
Than ever man loved, ever hated before—
And seek in the Valley of Love,
The nest, or the nook in Hate's Grove
Where my soul may surely reach
The essence, naught less, of each,
The Hate of all Hates, the Love
Of all Loves, in the Valley or Grove—
I find them the very warders
Each of the other's borders.

When I love most, Love is disguised
In Hate; and when Hate is surprised
In Love, then I hate most: ask
How Love smiles through Hate's iron casque,
Hate grins through Love's rose-braided mask,—
And how, having hated thee,
I sought long and painfully
To reach thy heart, nor prick
The skin but pierce to the quick—

—Pippa Passes

Dearest, three months ago
When we loved each other so,
Lived and loved the same
Till an evening came
When a shaft from the devil's bow
Pierced to our ingle-glow,
And the friends were friend and foe!

—A Lovers' Quarrel

Gone? All thwarts us.

—A Blot In the 'Scutcheon

⁂

He is with her, and they know that I know
Where they are, what they do: they believe
my tears flow
While they laugh, laugh at me

—The Laboratory

⁂

Unlearned love was safe from spurning—
Can't we respect your loveless learning?

—Christmas-Eve and Easter-Day

⁂

What's she? an infant save in heart and brain. Young!

—A Blot In the 'Scutcheon

O' Lyric Love, half angel and half bird,
And all a wonder and a wild desire,—
Boldest of hearts that ever braved the sun,
Took sanctuary within the holier blue,
And sang a kindred soul out to his face,—
Yet human at the red-ripe of the heart—
When the first summons from the darkling earth
Reached thee amid thy chambers, blanched their blue,
And bared them of the glory—to drop down,
To toil for man, to suffer or to die,—
This is the same voice: can thy soul know change?
Hail then, and hearken from the realms of help!
Never may I commence my song, my due
To God who best taught song by gift of thee,
Except with bent head and beseeching hand—
That still, despite the distance and the dark,
What was, again may be; some interchange
Of grace, some splendor once thy very thought,
Some benediction anciently thy smile:
—Never conclude, but raising hand and head
Thither where eyes, that cannot reach, yet yearn
For all hope, all sustainment, all reward,
Their upmost up and on,—so blessing back
In those thy realms of help, that heaven thy home,
Some whiteness which, I judge, thy face makes proud,
Some wanness where, I think, thy foot may fall!

—*The Ring and The Book*

In earnest, do you think I'd choose
That sort of new love to enslave me?
Mine should have lapped me round from the
        beginning;
As little fear of losing it as winning:
Lovers grow cold, men learn to hate their wives,
And only parents' love can last our lives.

—*Pippa Passes*

If you had pity on my passion, pity
On my protested sickness of the soul
To sit beside you, hear you breathe, and watch
Your eyelids and the eyes beneath—if you
Accorded gifts and knew not they were gifts—
If I grew mad at last with enterprise
And must behold my beauty in her bower
Or perish—(I was ignorant of even
My own desires—what then were you?) if sorrow—
Sin—if the end came—must I now renounce
My reason, blind myself to light, say truth
Is false and lie to God and my own soul?

—*A Blot In the 'Scutcheon*

I found God there, his visible power;
Yet felt in my heart, amid all its sense
Of the power, an equal evidence
That his love, there too, was the nobler dower.
For the loving worm within its clod,
Were diviner than a loveless god
Amid his worlds, I will dare to say.
You know what I mean: God's all, man's nought:
But also, God, whose pleasure brought
Man into being, stands away

—Christmas-Eve and Easter-Day

How she can lie!

—Pippa Passes

Gr-r-r—there go, my heart's abhorrence!
Water your damned flower-pots, do!

—Soliloquy of the Spanish Cloister

Sin has surprised us, so will punishment

—A Blot In the 'Scutcheon

How, forsooth, was I to know it
If Waring meant to glide away
Like a ghost at break of day?
Never looked he half so gay!

—Waring

Woman, and will you cast
For a word, quite off at last
Me, your own, your You,—
Since, as truth is true,
I was You all the happy past—
Me do you leave aghast
With the memories We amassed?

—A Lovers' Quarrel

Alone! I am left alone once more—

—*Christmas-Eve and Easter-Day*

That way you'd take, friend Austin? What a shame
I was your cousin, tamely from the first
Your bride, and all this fervour's run to waste!

—*A Blot In the 'Scutcheon*

Love's Regret

Then how grace a rose? I know a way!
Leave it, rather.
Must you gather?
Smell, kiss, wear it—at last, throw away!

—*A Pretty Woman*

Had she willed it, still had stood the screen
So slight, so sure, 'twixt my love and her:
I could fix her face with a guard between,
And find her soul as when friends confer,
Friends—lovers that might have been.

—*By the Fire-Side*

When I saw him tangled in her toils,
A shame, said I, if she adds just him
To her nine-and-ninety other spoils,
The hundredth for a whim!

—*A Light Woman*

In my own heart love had not been made wise
To trace love's faint beginnings in mankind,
To know even hate is but a mask of love's.
To see a good in evil, and a hope
In ill-success; to sympathize, be proud
Of their half-reasons, faint aspirings, dim
Struggles for truth, their poorest fallacies,
Their prejudice and fears and cares and doubts;
All with a touch of nobleness, despite
Their error, upward tending all though weak

—*Paracelsus*

And still, as love's brief morning wore,
With a gentle start, half smile, half sigh,
They found love not as it seemed before.

—*The Statue and the Bust*

But you don't know music! Wherefore
Keep on casting pearls
To a—poet? All I care for
Is—to tell him that a girl's
"Love" comes aptly in when gruff
Grows his singing. (There, enough!)

—A Tale

But do not let us quarrel any more

—Andrea del Sarto

Is the knowledge of her, naught? the memory,
naught?
—Lady, should such an one have looked on you,
Ne'er wrong yourself so far as quote the world
And say, love can go unrequited here!
You will have blessed him to his whole life's end—
Low passions hindered, baser cares kept back,
All goodness cherished where you dwelt—and dwell.

—Colombe's Birthday

I think then, I should wish to stand
This evening in that dear, lost land,
Over the sea the thousand miles,
And know if yet that woman smiles
With the calm smile; some little farm
She lives in there, no doubt: what harm
If I sat on the door-side bench,
And, while her spindle made a trench
Fantastically in the dust,
Inquired of all her fortunes—just
Her children's ages and their names,
And what may be the husband's aims
For each of them. I'd talk this out,
And sit there, for an hour about,
Then kiss her hand once more, and lay
Mine on her head, and go my way.

—*The Italian In England*

Over?
Oh, what is over? what must I live through
And say, "'tis over"? Is our meeting over?
Have I received in presence of them all
The partner of my guilty love—with brow
Trying to seem a maiden's brow—with lips
Which make believe that when they strive to form
Replies to you and tremble as they strive

—*A Blot In the 'Scutcheon*

But you spared me this, like the heart you are,
And filled my empty heart at a word.
If two lives join, there is oft a scar,
They are one and one, with a shadowy third;
One near one is too far.

—*By the Fire-Side*

Good, to forgive;
Best, to forget!
Living, we fret;
Dying, we live.
Fretless and free,
Soul, clap thy pinion!
Earth have dominion,
Body, o'er thee!

Wander at will,
Day after day—
Wander away,
Wandering still—
Soul that canst soar!
Body may slumber:
Body shall cumber
Soul-flight no more.

Waft of soul's wing!
What lies above?
Sunshine and Love,
Skyblue and Spring!
Body hides—where?
Ferns of all feather,
Mosses and heather.
Yours be the care!

—Good to Forgive

Love's Regret

Let's contend no more, Love,
    Strive nor weep:
All be as before, Love,
    —Only sleep!

            —*A Woman's Last Word*

⁂

All's over, then: does truth sound bitter
    As one at first believes?
Hark, 'tis the sparrows' good-night twitter
    About your cottage eaves!

And the leaf-buds on the vine are woolly,
    I noticed that, to-day;
One day more bursts them open fully
    —You know the red turns grey.

To-morrow we meet the same then, dearest?
    May I take your hand in mine?
Mere friends are we,—well, friends the merest
    Keep much that I resign:

For each glance of the eye so bright and black,
Though I keep with heart's endeavour,—
Your voice, when you wish the snowdrops back,
Though it stay in my soul for ever!—

Yet I will but say what mere friends say,
Or only a thought stronger;
I will hold your hand but as long as all may,
Or so very little longer!

—The Lost Mistress

How could it end in any other way?

—Andrea del Sarto

I loved you, Evelyn, all the while.
My heart seemed full as it could hold?

—Evelyn Hope

That way you'd take, friend Austin? What a shame
I was your cousin, tamely from the first
Your bride, and all this fervour's run to waste!

—A Blot In the 'Scutcheon

Young-hearted women, old-minded men

—The Flight of the Duchess

I seem to see! We meet and part; 'tis brief

—Any Wife to Any Husband

Would he loved me yet,
On and on,
While I found some way undreamed
—Paid my debt!
Gave more life and more,
Till, all gone

—In a Year

All June I bound the rose in sheaves.
Now, rose by rose, I strip the leaves
And strew them where Pauline may pass.
She will not turn aside? Alas!
Let them lie. Suppose they die?
The chance was they might take her eye.

How many a month I strove to suit
These stubborn fingers to the lute!
To-day I venture all I know.
She will not hear my music? So!
Break the string; fold music's wing:
Suppose Pauline had bade me sing!

My whole life long I learned to love.
This hour my utmost art I prove
And speak my passion—heaven or hell?
She will not give me heaven? 'Tis well!
Lose who may—I still can say,
Those who win heaven, blest are they!

—*One Way of Love*

I earned no more by a warble
Than you by a sketch in plaster;
You wanted a piece of marble,
I needed a music-master.

—*Youth and Art*

Dearest, three months ago
When the mesmerizer Snow
With his hand's first sweep
Put the earth to sleep:
'Twas a time when the heart could show
All—how was earth to know,
'Neath the mute hand's to-and-fro?

—*A Lovers' Quarrel*

What need to strive with a life awry?
Had I said that, had I done this,
So might I gain, so might I miss.
Might she have loved me? just as well
She might have hated, who can tell!
Where had I been now if the worst befell?

—The Last Ride Together

The counter our lovers staked was lost
As surely as if it were lawful coin:
And the sin I impute to each frustrate ghost
Is—the unlit lamp and the ungirt loin,
Though the end in sight was a vice, I say.
You of the virtue (we issue join)
How strive you? *De te, fabula.*

—The Statue and the Bust

She followed down to the sea-shore;
I left and never saw her more.

—The Italian In England

There may be heaven; there must be hell;
Meantime, there is our earth here—well!

—Time's Revenges

Love, to be wise . . .
Should we have—months ago, when first we loved

—Pippa Passes

Into her very hair, back swerving
Over each shoulder, loose and abundant,
As her head thrown back showed the white throat
curving;
And the very tresses shared in the pleasure,
Moving to the mystic measure,
Bounding as the bosom bounded.
I stopped short, more and more confounded

—The Flight of the Duchess

Sitting by my side,
At my feet,
So he breathed but air I breathed,
Satisfied!
I, too, at love's brim
Touched the sweet

—*In a Year*

Loving is done with. Were he sitting now,
As so few hours since, on that seat, we'd love
No more—contrive no thousand happy ways
To hide love from the loveless, any more.

—*A Blot In the 'Scutcheon*

But you meet the Prince at the Board,
I'm queen myself at *bals-paré*,
I've married a rich old lord,
And you're dubbed knight and an R.A.

Each life unfulfilled, you see;
It hangs still, patchy and scrappy:
We have not sighed deep, laughed free,
Starved, feasted, despaired,—been happy.

And nobody calls you a dunce,
And people suppose me clever:
This could but have happened once,
And we missed it, lost it for ever.

—Youth and Art

I should have gone home again,
Kissed Jacynth, and soberly drowned myself!

—The Flight of the Duchess

Oh, Mildred, feel you not
That now, while I remember every glance
Of yours, each word of yours, with power to test
And weigh them in the diamond scales of pride

—A Blot In the 'Scutcheon

"Not my hair!" made the girl her moan—
"All the rest is gone or to go;
But the last, last grace, my all, my own,
Let it stay in the grave, that the ghosts may know!
Leave my poor gold hair alone!"

The passion thus vented, dead lay she;
Her parents sobbed their worst on that;
All friends joined in, nor observed degree:
For indeed the hair was to wonder at,
As it spread—not flowing free,

But curled around her brow, like a crown,
And coiled beside her cheeks, like a cap,
And calmed about her neck—ay, down
To her breast, pressed flat, without a gap
I' the gold, it reached her gown.

All kissed that face, like a silver wedge
'Mid the yellow wealth, nor disturbed its hair:
E'en the priest allowed death's privilege,
As he planted the crucifix with care
On her breast, 'twixt edge and edge.

—*Gold Hair*

So weeks grew months, years; gleam by gleam
The glory dropped from their youth and love,
And both perceived they had dreamed a dream.

—The Statue and the Bust

Alas,
We loved, sir—used to meet:
How sad and bad and mad it was—
But then, how it was sweet!

—Confessions

Mildred, break it if you choose,
A heart the love of you uplifted—still
Uplifts, thro' this protracted agony,
To heaven! but Mildred, answer me

—A Blot In the 'Scutcheon

But love, love, love—there's better love, I know!
This foolish love was only day's first offer;
I choose my next love to defy the scoffer

—In Three Days

So, saying like Eve when she plucked the apple,
"I wanted a taste, and now there's enough of it"

—Christmas-Eve and Easter-Day

Meantime, how much I loved him,
I find out now I've lost him.
I who cared not if I moved him,
Who could so carelessly accost him,
Henceforth never shall get free
Of his ghostly company

—Waring

All traces of the rough forbidden path
My rash love lured her to! Each day must see
Some fear of hers effaced, some hope renewed:
Then there will be surprises, unforeseen
Delights in store. I'll not regret the past.

—A Blot In the 'Scutcheon

Memory
of Love

Memory of Love

We would try and trace
One another's face
In the ash, as an artist draws;
Free on each other's flaws,
How we chattered like two church daws!

—A Lovers' Quarrel

And oh, all my heart how it loved him!

—Saul

So grew my own small life complete,
As nature obtained her best of me—
One born to love you, sweet!

—By the Fire-Side

And when, shortly after, she carried
Her shame from the Court, and they married

—The Glove

But the soul
Whence the love comes, all ravage leaves that whole;
Vainly the flesh fades; soul makes all things new.

—Any Wife to Any Husband

No sooner the old hope goes to ground
Than a new one, straight to the self-same mark

—Life in a Love

How the world is made for each of us!
How all we perceive and know in it

—By the Fire-Side

That's my last Duchess painted on the wall,
Looking as if she were alive.

—My Last Duchess

Dearest, three months ago!
When we lived blocked-up with snow,—
When the wind would edge
In and in his wedge,
In, as far as the point could go—
Not to our ingle, though,
Where we loved each the other so!

—A Lovers' Quarrel

Love, you did give all I asked

—Andrea del Sarto

Come back with me to the first of all,
Let us lean and love it over again,
Let us now forget and now recall,
Break the rosary in a pearly rain,
And gather what we let fall!

—By the Fire-Side

One likes to show the truth for the truth;
That the woman was light is very true

—A Light Woman

One lyric woman, in her crocus vest
Woven of sea-wools, with her two white hands
Commends to me the strainer and the cup
Thy lip hath bettered ere it blesses mine.

—Cleon

My perfect wife, my Leonor,
Oh heart, my own, oh eyes, mine too,
Whom else could I dare look backward for,
With whom beside should I dare pursue
The path grey heads abhor?

—By the Fire-Side

No, indeed! for God above
Is great to grant, as mighty to make,
And creates the love to reward the love:
I claim you still, for my own love's sake!

—Evelyn Hope

Say again, what we are?
The sprite of a star,
I lure thee above where the destinies bar
My plumes their full play
Till a ruddier ray
Than my pale one announce there is withering away
Some . . . Scatter the vision for ever! And now,
As of old, I am I, thou art thou!

—In a Gondola

Was it something said,
Something done,
Vexed him? was it touch of hand,
Turn of head?
Strange! that very way
Love begun:
I as little understand
Love's decay.

—*In a Year*

What does it all mean, poet? Well,
Your brains beat into rhythm, you tell
What we felt only; you expressed
You hold things beautiful the best,
And pace them in rhyme so, side by side.
'Tis something, nay 'tis much: but then,
Have you yourself what's best for men?

—*The Last Ride Together*

144

For life, with all it yields of joy and woe,
And hope and fear,—believe the aged friend,—
Is just our chance o' the prize of learning love,
How love might be, hath been indeed, and is

—A Death in the Desert

Thy singleness of soul that made me proud,
Thy purity of heart I loved aloud,
Thy man's-truth I was bold to bid God see!

—Any Wife to Any Husband

For there I picked up on the heather
And there I put inside my breast
A moulted feather, an eagle-feather!
Well, I forget the rest.

—Memorabilia

Dear, the pang is brief,
Do thy part,
Have thy pleasure! How perplexed
Grows belief!
Well, this cold clay clod
Was man's heart:
Crumble it, and what comes next?
Is it God?

—*In a Year*

All, that I know
Of a certain star
Is, it can throw
(Like the angled spar)
Now a dart of red,
Now a dart of blue;
Till my friends have said
They would fain see, too,
My star that dartles the red and the blue!
Then it stops like a bird; like a flower, hangs furled:
They must solace themselves with the Saturn above it.
What matter to me if their star is a world?
Mine has opened its soul to me; therefore I love it.

—*My Star*

God be thanked, the meanest of his creatures
Boasts two soul-sides, one to face the world with,
One to show a woman when he loves her.

—*One Word More*

What Youth deemed crystal,
Age find out was dew

—*Jochanan Hakkadosh*

All I can say is—I saw it!
The room was as bare as your hand.
I locked in the swarth little lady,—I swear,
From the head to the foot of her—well, quite as bare!
"No Nautch shall cheat me," said I, "taking my stand
At this bolt which I draw!" And this bolt—
I withdraw it,
And there laughs the lady, not bare, but embowered
With—who knows what verdure, o'erfruited,
o'erflowered?
Impossible! Only—I saw it!

All I can sing is—I feel it!
This life was as blank as that room;
I let you pass in here. Precaution, indeed?
Walls, ceiling and floor,—not a chance for a weed!
Wide opens the entrance: where's cold, now, where's
gloom?
No May to sow seed here, no June to reveal it,
Behold you enshrined in these blooms of your
bringing,
These fruits of your bearing—nay, birds of your
winging!
A fairy-tale! Only—I feel it!

—*Natural Magic*

I had a lover—shame avaunt!
This poor wrenched body, grim and gaunt,
Was kissed all over till it burned,
By lips the truest, love e'er turned

—*The Confessional*

And thus was she buried, inviolate
Of body and soul, in the very space
By the altar; keeping saintly state
In Pornic church, for her pride of race,
Pure life and piteous fate.

And in after-time would your fresh tear fall,
Though your mouth might twitch with a dubious
smile,
As they told you of gold, both robe and pall,
How she prayed them leave it alone awhile,
So it never was touched at all.

Years flew; this legend grew at last
The life of the lady; all she had done,
All been, in the memories fading fast
Of lover and friend, was summed in one
Sentence survivors passed

—*Gold Hair*

To say, 'What matters it at the end?
I did no more while my heart was warm
Than does that image, my pale-faced friend.'

—The Statue and the Bust

Take and keep my fifty poems finished;
Where my heart lies, let my brain lie also!

—One Word More

If since eve drew in, I say,
I have sat and brought
(So to speak) my thought
To bear on the woman away,
Till I felt my hair turn grey—

Till I seemed to have and hold,
In the vacancy
'Twixt the wall and me

—Mesmerism

"Love conquers all things." What love conquers
them?
I mean, and should have said, whose love is best
Of all that love or that profess to love?
True love.

—*A Blot In the 'Scutcheon*

Dear, had the world in its caprice
Deigned to proclaim "I know you both,
Have recognized your plighted troth,
Am sponsor for you: live in peace!"—
How many precious months and years
Of youth had passed, that speed so fast,
Before we found it out at last,
The world, and what it fears?

How much of priceless life were spent
With men that every virtue decks,
And women models of their sex,
Society's true ornament,—
Ere we dared wander, nights like this,
Thro' wind and rain, and watch the Seine,
And feel the Boulevard break again
To warmth and light and bliss?

I know! the world proscribes not love;
　　Allows my finger to caress
　　Your lips' contour and downiness,
　　Provided it supply a glove.
The world's good word—the Institute!
　　Guizot receives Montalembert!
Eh? Down the court three lampions flare:
　　Put forward your best foot!

—Respectability

Yet we called out—"Depart!
Our gifts, once given, must here abide.
Our work is done; we have no heart
To mar our work,"—we cried.

—Over the Sea Our Galleys Went

That, they might spare; a certain wood
Might miss the plant; their loss were small:
But I—whene'er the leaf grows there,
Its drop comes from my heart, that's all.

—*May and Death*

To wit, she was meant for heaven, not earth;
Had turned an angel before the time:
Yet, since she was mortal, in such dearth
Of frailty, all you could count a crime
Was—she knew her gold hair's worth.

—*Gold Hair*

Verse-making was least of my virtues:
I viewed with despair
Wealth that never yet was but might be—
all that verse-making were
If the life would but lengthen to wish, let
the mind be laid bare.
So I said, "To do little is bad, to do nothing is worse"—
And made verse.

Love-making,—how simple a matter!
No depths to explore,
No heights in a life to ascend! No
disheartening Before,
No affrighting Hereafter,—love now will be
love ever more.
So I felt "To keep silence were folly:"—
all language above,
I made love.

—Ferishtah's Fancies

Take away love, and our earth is a tomb!

—Fra Lippo Lippi

Love's Letters

To Elizabeth Barrett Browning

I do not, nor will not think, dearest, of ever 'making you happy'—I can imagine no way of working that end, which does not go straight to my own truest, only true happiness—yet in every such effort there is implied some distinction, some supererogatory grace, or why speak of it at all? You it is, are my happiness, and all that ever can be: YOU—dearest!

But never, if you would not, what you will not do I know, never revert to *that* frightful wish. 'Disappoint me?' 'I speak what I know and testify what I have seen'—you shall 'mystery' again and again—I do not dispute that, but do not *you* dispute, neither, that mysteries are. But it is simply because I do most justice to the mystical part of what I feel for you, because I consent to lay most stress on that fact of facts that I love you, beyond admiration, and respect, and esteem and affection even, and do not adduce any reason which stops short of accounting for *that*, whatever else it would account for, because I do this, in pure logical justice—you are able to turn and wonder (if you do . . . *now*) what causes it all! My love, only wait, only believe in me, and it cannot be but I shall, little by little, become known to you—after long years, perhaps, but still one day: I *would* say *this* now—but I will write more to-morrow. God bless my sweetest—ever, love, I am your
R.B.

***

I will not try and write much to-night, dearest, for my head gives a little warning—and I have so much to think

of!—spite of my penholder being kept back from me after all!
Now, ought I to have asked for it? Or did I not seem grateful
enough at the promise? This last would be a characteristic
reason, seeing that I reproached myself with feeling too
grateful for the 'special symbol'—the 'essential meaning' of
which was already in my soul. Well then, I will—I do pray
for it—next time; and I will keep it for that one yesterday
and all its memories—and it shall bear witness against me,
if, on the Siren's isle, I grow forgetful of Wimpole Street.
And when is 'next time' to be—Wednesday or Thursday?
When I look back on the strangely steady widening of my
horizon—how no least interruption has occurred to visits
or letters—oh, care *you*, sweet—care for us both!

That remark of your sister's delights me—you
remember?—that the anger would not be so formidable. I
have exactly the fear of encountering *that*, which the sense
of having to deal with a ghost would induce: there's no
striking at it with one's partizan. Well, God is above all! It is
not my fault if it so happens that by returning my love you
make me exquisitely blessed; I believe—more than hope, I
am *sure* I should do all I ever *now* can do, if you were never
to know it—that is, my love for you was in the first instance
its own reward—if one must use such phrases—and if it
were possible for that . . . not *anger*, which is of no good,
but that *opposition*—that adverse will—to show that your
good would be attained by the—

But it would need to be *shown* to me. You have said
thus to me—in the very last letter, indeed. But with me,
or any *man*, the instincts of happiness develop themselves
too unmistakably where there is anything like a freedom of
will. The man whose heart is set on being rich or influential
after the worldly fashion, may be found far enough from
the attainment of either riches or influence—but he will be

in the presumed way to them—pumping at the pump, if he is really anxious for water, even though the pump be dry—but not sitting still by the dusty roadside.

I believe—first of all, you—but when that is done, and I am allowed to call your heart *mine*,—I cannot think you would be happy if parted from me—and *that* belief, coming to add to my own feeling in *that* case. So, this *will* be—I trust in God.

In life, in death, I am your own, *my* own! My head has got well already! It is so slight a thing, that I make such an ado about! Do not reply to these bodings—they are gone—they seem absurd! All steps secured but the last, and that last the easiest! Yes—far easiest! For first you had to be created, only that; and then, in my time; and then, not in Timbuctoo but Wimpole Street, and then ... the strange hedge round the sleeping Palace keeping the world off—and then . . . all was to begin, all the difficulty only *begin*:—and now . . . see where is reached! And I kiss you, and bless you, my dearest, in earnest of the end!

R. B.

***

I am altogether your own, dearest—the words were only words and the playful feelings were play—while the *fact* has always been so irresistibly obvious as to make them *break* on and off it, fantastically like water turning to spray and spurts of foam on a great solid rock. *Now* you call the rock, a rock, but you must have known what chance you had of pushing it down when you sent all those light fancies and free-leaves, and refusals-to-hold-responsible, to do what they could. It *is* a rock; and may be quite barren of good to you,—not large enough to build houses on, not small enough to make a mantelpiece of, much less a pedestal for a statue, but it is real rock, that is all.

It is always *I* who 'torment' you—instead of taking the present and blessing you, and leaving the future to its own cares. I certainly am not apt to look curiously into what next week is to bring, much less next month or six months, but you, the having you, my own, dearest beloved, *that* is as different in kind as in degree from any other happiness or semblance of it that even seemed possible of realization. Then, now, the health is all to stay, or retard us—oh, be well, my Ba!

R.B.

***

Dear, dear Ba, but indeed I *did* return home earlier by two or three good hours than the night before—and to find *no* letter,—none of yours! *That* was reserved for this morning early, and then a rest came, a silence, over the thoughts of you—and now again, comes this last note! Oh, my love—why—what is it you think to do, or become 'afterward,' that you may fail in and so disappoint me? It is not very unfit that you should thus punish yourself, and that, sinning by your own ambition of growing something beyond my Ba even, you should 'fear' as you say! For, sweet, why wish, why think to alter ever by a line, change by a shade, turn better if that were possible, and so only rise the higher above me, get further from instead of nearer to my heart? What I expect, what I build my future on, am quite, quite prepared to 'risk' everything for,—is that one belief that you *will not alter*, will just remain as you are—meaning by '*you*,' the love in you, the qualities I have *known* (for you will stop me, if I do not stop myself) what

I have evidence of in every letter, in every word, every look. Keeping these, if it be God's will that the body passes,— what is that? Write no new letters, speak no new words, look no new looks,—only tell me, years hence that the present is alive, that what was once, still is—and I am, must needs be, blessed as ever! You speak of my feeling as if it were a pure speculation—as if because I *see somewhat* in you I make a calculation that there must be more to see somewhere or other—where bdellium is found, the onyx-stone may be looked for in the mystic land of the four rivers! And perhaps . . . ah, poor human nature!—perhaps I *do* think at times on what *may* be to find! But what is that to you? I *offer* for the bdellium—the other may be found or not found . . . what I see glitter on the ground, *that* will suffice to make me rich as—rich as—

So bless you my own Ba! I would not wait for paper, and you must forgive half-sheets, instead of a whole celestial quire to my love and praise. Are you so well? So adventurous? Thank you from my heart of hearts. And I am quite well to-day (and have received a note from Procter *just* this *minute* putting off his dinner on account of the death of his wife's sister's husband abroad). Observe *this* sheet I take as I find—I mean, that the tear tells of no improper speech repented of—what English, what sense, what a soul's tragedy! but then, what real, realest love and more than love for my ever dearest Ba possesses her own—

R.B.

* * *

How will the love my heart is full of for you, let me be silent? Insufficient speech is better than no speech, in one regard—the speaker had *tried* words, and if they fail, hereafter he needs not reflect that he did not even try—so with me now, that loving you, Ba, with all my heart and soul, all my senses being lost in one wide wondering gratitude and veneration, I press close to you to say so, in this imperfect way, my dear dearest beloved! Why do you not help me, rather than take my words, my proper word, from me and call them yours, when yours they are not? You said lately love of you 'made you humble'—just as if to hinder *me* from saying that earnest truth!—entirely true it is, as I feel ever more convincingly. You do not choose to understand it should be so, nor do I much care, for the one thing you must believe, must resolve to believe in its length and breadth, is that I do love you and live only in the love of you.

I will rest on the confidence that you do so believe! You *know* by this that it is no shadowy image of you and *not* you, which having attached myself to in the first instance, I afterward compelled my fancy to see reproduced, so to speak, with tolerable exactness to the original idea, in you, the dearest real *you* I am blessed with—you *know* what the eyes are to me, and the lips and the hair. And I, for my part, know *now*, while fresh from seeing you, certainly *know*, whatever I may have said a short time since, that *you* will go on to the end, that the arm round me will not let me go,—over such a blind abyss—I refuse to think, to fancy, *towards* what it would be to loose you now! So I give my life, my soul into your hand—the giving is a mere form too, it is yours, ever yours from the first—but ever as I see you, sit with you, and come away to think over it all, I find more that seems mine to give; you give me more life and it goes back to you.

I shall hear from you to-morrow—then, I will go out early and get done with some calls, in the joy and consciousness of what waits me, and when I return I will write a few words. Are these letters, these merest attempts at getting to talk with you through the distance—yet always with the consolation of feeling that you will know all, interpret all and forgive it and put it right—can such things be cared for, expected, as you say? Then, Ba, my life *must* be better . . . with the closeness to help, and the 'finding out the way' for which love was always noted. If you begin making in fancy a lover to your mind, I am lost at once—but the one quality of *affection* for you, which would sooner or later have to be placed on his list of component graces; *that* I will dare start supply—the entire love you could dream of *is* here. You think you see some of the other adornments, and only too many; and you will see plainer one day, but with that I do not concern myself—you shall admire the true heroes—but me you shall love for the love's sake. Let me kiss you, you, my dearest, dearest—God bless you ever—

R.B.